AF413861

100 POEMS FOR 100 YEARS
A POETRY MEMOIR

MURIEL FISCHER HOFF
1923-2023

100 POEMS FOR 100 YEARS
A POETRY MEMOIR

MURIEL FISCHER HOFF
1923-2023

Editor & Publisher   David Michael Hoff

To request permission for making copies of
any printed material please contact:
David Michael Hoff
dhoff@sbcglobal.net
david47hoff@icloud.com

<u>Poetry Books Of Muriel Hoff</u>

Animal Alphabet Rhymes For Children Up To Ninety

Messages Via Muriel

The Voice In The Middle Of The Night

Inspired Poems From The Universe

Chosen To Channel

Waterfall Of Love

Beautiful The Whispering Of Wind

Between God and me

<u>Muriel Hoff Poetry Appears In These Anthologies</u>

More Than Magnolias

Writers' Choice

Women Of The Piedmont Triad

Edge Of Our World

A Turn In Time

The Voice Within

Wordworks

Fire And Chocolate

Soundings Of Poetry

North Carolina's 400 Years

Signs Along The Way

Here's To The Land

Dad and Mom

George & Muriel

Acknowledgments

First and foremost, I owe a debt of gratitude and appreciation to my brother Stephen for believing in this book project.
He graciously offered to finance the entire costs.

I would like to extend a shout out of thanks to Roger Adler, the book's proofreader par excellence.

Over the years Wendy Byerly and the staff of Minuteman Press of High Point, North Carolina have helped tremendously through their advice and expertise.

Foreword

I can fondly remember the multitude of times my mother would tell me how she longed for and thought of writing her own memoir. Alas, life always would get in the way for one reason or another and it never happened. Yet, she continued to talk of a memoir even until the last months of life.

Although this is the ninth published book of her writings, none before were personal and up-close looks into her life, thoughts, and emotions. I think she would be happy with this work since it zeros in on her likes and dislikes, her values and morals, and her family and friends. I hope this book brings to you a small and special sampling of her works.

I also hope she would be proud of this as her memoir.

David M. Hoff

TABLE OF CONTENTS

AN INTRODUCTION

Let's start out with five poems.

<u>WHEN LADY DAY SANG THE BLUES</u>

"This is a poem memoir I wrote which took place at the end of World War 11. It is in a famous Manhattan nightclub where the fabulous singer Billie Holiday performed. The event changed my life."

When Lady Day sang the blues above the smoky haze,

the Cafe Society became a cathedral of soul.

When she sang of love, I felt lovely.

When she sang of loneliness I felt lonely.

Pure passion sprung from those lips.

The blue notes bounced along

with the wail of the saxophone,

and the plinking of the ivories

carrying me along a rushing current.

That night George sported his Navy uniform,

and I wore a rhinestone-studded powder blue dress.

During the break George pulled from his pocket

a box of licorice cigarettes, my weakness.

Underneath something glittered.

He ceremoniously placed the diamond ring

on my finger and said, "Now we are engaged."

After the break when Billie sang the blues,

all I could hear was the pounding of my heart.

All I could see was the diamond sparkling

in the flickering candlelight, and all I could

feel were his fingers entwined with mine.

THE PROPOSAL IN 1945
Muriel wrote this about her fiancé George's proposal.

George's letter on the mahogany drum table,

the words staring up at me.

"I'll call early Tuesday, April 12th…

may have important news for you."

I pictured him in his Navy whites,

long lanky frame,

searching eyes that sometimes smile,

making confrontation disappear.

The spring rain splattered my window,

a staccato beat matching the drumming

of my fingers on the mahogany table.

Shrill ringing, the telephone pierced the moment.

"Honey…sorry couldn't get through,

the lines were jammed.

Did you know Roosevelt died?
The new guy, Truman…
from Missouri, I hear."

Like a flashback from an old movie,
I could see my mother at the kitchen table
checkered apron, black hair braided into a tiara,
green eyes blazing, rhapsodizing on Roosevelt.

"The Depression people selling apples on
street corners, breadlines, begging.
Roosevelt created jobs, the WPA, REA…
truly a miracle worker."

The past slipped away Roosevelt was dead…
we were at war.
Who would lead us to victory?
Speechless, heart pounding, hands clammy,
the phone pressed to my ear, I felt limp.

"Muriel, are you there? Talk to me.

I gotta take a draft of men up to Newport.

How about getting married?"

George's proposal… I felt transfused, energized.

"George darling yes, yes, yes.

I would be proud and happy to be your wife."

I had three days. Too late for invitations,

telephone calls would work.

The city would be paralyzed mourning

a beloved president, businesses closed.

Somewhere in New York

there must be a rabbi, a wedding dress.

<u>FOR LOVERS ONLY</u>
Written by Muriel after marriage.

All young couples like to coo

in a movie theater for a dollar or two.

Their heads together, their hands entwined,

as to seeing the picture— why love is blind!

All young couples like to spoon,

whenever they get a slice of the moon.

Just give them a spot that's sufficiently dark,

and pronto, they kindle that well-known spark.

All young couples like to neck

whenever they can, they don't give a heck.

At date time the gal is smoother than ice,

her hair is so perfect, her makeup so nice.

At the end of the evening when the love light is spent,

both of them feel so solidly sent.

The gal peeks in her mirror, "My God! I'm a wreck."

This is the result of a three-hour neck.

History books from days of yore

had chapters on ladies who knew the score.

Down through the ages it's never changed.

The names are different, but the object's the same.

So on reading this poem, let the moral be

to follow your feelings, don't stifle the flame.

You may end up in the Hall Of Fame.

* spoon—to cuddle
* price of a movie in late 1940s —one or two dollars

AMERICA THE GOLDEN

This biographical sketch is about Muriel's mother-in-law Lena, or Leincha in Polish. Lena came to America at age 13 in the early 1900s.

Rabbi Verbal of Cracow tugged at his beard.

His eyes, living black coals, thoughtfully flitted

from his wife Hannah, anxiously twisting the corners

of her apron, to his youngest daughter,

Leincha, tears streaming down her lovely face.

Hannah said, "Samuel, this girl is only a child.

She is not ready for marriage."

Samuel spoke back, "You were married at fifteen

and at age sixteen were with child."

"My husband, Leincha is different. Across the ocean,

drums of freedom call."

"But Hannah, liebchen, I saved for the dowry, made

arrangements for the marriage, and with such a

fine scholar, the son of Rabbi Isadore Ben Levi."

Lena broke in, "Father I beg you, let me go

with Tante Becky to America. I have to seek my own
fortune, my own love. In the Talmud it says a woman
prefers poverty with love to riches without love.
Cut the strings, set me free."

Rabbi Verbel closed his eyes in contemplation,
rocking to and fro seeking guidance from within.
He said, "Leincha, my dear, God creates each being
uniquely bestowing the gift of free choice.
My heart cries out, "My child, stay! But a small still voice
answers, 'let her go.' Here is your dowry, use it wisely and
remember who you are and where you came from.
Go in honor with God's blessing, shalom."

Leincha left the shtetl in Cracow, Poland, for America,
but the only gold she found was in Aunt Becky's teeth.
She had to sleep in the pantry with Basha,
who smelled and jumped with fleas.
Aunt Becky awakened Leincha early in the morning,

shaking her by the shoulders.

She said "Get up Leincha put my rouge on your cheeks
and I'll give you some lipstick. Go down to Belty's
Dress Factory. They pay $3.00 a week, and then you can
pay me $1.00 for your board."

That night Leincha fell asleep exhausted.
In a dream she saw a big room filled with sewing
machines and bobbins of many-colored threads.
They were moving and calling her name,
"Leincha, Leincha, Leincha."

THE PILL
Written December 20, 1966

What has caused a sexual revolution,

    giving doctors problems to ponder?

Turned Mama into a femme fatale,

    from up North to way down yonder.

        THE PILL!

What's come over the woman, who used to complain,

    she was tired and ill at ease?

Now she's ready for love at all hours,

    despite Dad's feeble pleas.

        THE PILL!

Where oh where has my little wife gone,

    who never would stray from the home?

I refused her last night and we had a fight.

    Why does my little wife roam?

        THE PILL!

Why is my manhood up at stake?

    Instead of sex—can't she bake a cake,

or take a cold shower like I used to do.

    Give me a hint, one little clue.

      THE PILL!

Why is she determined to wear me out?

    When I can do with or without.

      THE PILL!

PART ONE

POETRY OF AMERICA

Muriel expressed in writing her strong support of America and the ideals of the country. In the following five writings she addresses some of her thoughts and feelings.

-

SALUTE AMERICAN VETERANS

American veterans deserve your support.

Think of all the battles they have fought.

They suffered wounds to honor our nation.

Stand up for veterans, repair their foundation.

Thank our wounded veterans by being a volunteer.

Visit patients, be a caregiver, show how you care.

Thank wounded heroes for all they have done

in fighting for America, and the battles they have won.

<u>PRIDE IN THE U.S.A.</u>

How proud am I to be

living in the land of the free.

We are all citizens in the U.S.A.

and we are all special in our own way.

How blessed to live in a democracy

and discover our individuality.

If you prove the value of who you are

you can rise to be a shining star.

America, the treasure we hold most dear,

fills my heart with pride, erases my fear.

There is equal opportunity, be brave and strive.

We are all citizens of America, happy to be alive.

THE PRESIDENT OF THE UNITED STATES

The President sits alone in his chair,

his hand to his head in deep despair.

His furrowed brow reveals his plight,

another decision to be made tonight.

"When I was a boy I thought life would be

as easy as chopping down a cherry tree.

But the path was thorny, long and winding.

Yet, I looked and listened and soon was finding,

that many a door would open for me,

till the final door—the Presidency."

"Many were the friends I made over the years,

who saw me through the joys and tears,

who helped me legislate many a bill,

who helped me a quorum fill."

"They say I've twisted many an arm.

They say I really put on the charm.

I'm a politician—can't you see?

My aim in life —the Presidency."

And now he sits in his chair alone,

the decisions he makes are his very own.

Time will tell the rest.

If his decisions were the very best.

Within his heart he knows he tried

to do what was right to turn the tide.

And after all is said and done,

the blame —or the glory—rests on one.

The President is the President!

THE WARS

The young man wears a uniform

to whom does he owe his allegiance?

Why is he fighting?

Which war is this one?

Oh mothers of the night,

your cries reach out all over the world.

LET MY CHILDREN GO!

LET WARS CEASE!

LET LOVE INVADE THE BORDERS OF

MEN'S HEARTS, AND HOLD THEM PRISONERS

SO THEIR THOUGHTS TURN NOT TO PLUNDER!

THANKSGIVING 1979

We give thanks for nature's bounty,

for freedoms our fathers fought for

and bequeathed unto our children.

To share together Thanksgiving

with pride and joy of living

for our heritage America.

PART TWO

COMMENTARY WRITINGS

Muriel often wrote a commentary poem because she had been moved by a newspaper article, a television news piece, or a magazine essay. The next six poem/writings were such works.

THE SILENT SENATOR
From an article in the *Greensboro Daily News.*

Please call me by my name, that is Senator.

The Silent Senator they call me.

Why?

I reckon it's because I hold the record for silence.

One hundred sixteen days—an entire session.

Did I ever have any questions?

Sure sonny, but I figured if I kept quiet

those senator-lawyers would speak long enough

to clear up the confusion.

If they could stay away from the television cameras.

My biggest problem is not speaking, but thinking.

I try to avoid the confusion, but it's mighty difficult.

Many is the time I have voted—confused.

Not to get off the subject, but one thing I'm mighty

proud of is winning all those attendance prizes.

Electric clocks, boxes of chocolate, carving sets,

and then a book on the Revolutionary War.

Hmm—I wonder what kind of prizes

they'll be having next year?

THE HANGING OF GEORGE CARPENTER

Did you hear how they hung George Carpenter

back in 1875?

They strung him up—so the legend goes,

but George Carpenter never died!

The rope they cut real quick,

the coffin it was ready.

They put him in and galloped off

in a wagon not so steady.

Maybe God knew George was innocent

and not a murdering cheat.

For He was at the hanging

when George fell to his feet.

Rumor had it that George escaped,

and a log lay in his coffin.

There were those who swore he didn't die.

Yea, they talked about him often.

After 84 years of waiting

his kinfolk opened the grave.

They smiled as they looked at that moldy log.

For their George, the good Lord did save.

THE RAINBOW THAT MADE A BIG DIFFERENCE

He stood on the seventh floor ledge.

From the open window he could hear

the policeman pleading, "Mr. Jacobs don't

jump—it's a long way down."

Then his wife Carol's voice, "Harry I can't go on

without you. We can work it out as long as

we have each other."

He dangled one foot over the ledge,

and Carol's shrill scream penetrated his ears.

The cars and trucks in the street were miniature toys,

and the people were Barbie and Ken lookalikes.

Faintly he could hear them yelling "Jump, jump."

Instantly the cruelty and inhumanity of the crowd

pierced his heart.

He yelled, "If I jump, it will be on your conscience."

The chorus continued uninterrupted,

a monotonous wave of malevolence.

A sudden burst of rain almost made him lose balance.

Then the sun broke through followed by

a spectacular rainbow which seemed so close

he could reach out and touch it.

Standing at the beginning of the rainbow

were his mom and dad.

He watched in awe as they spoke to him

in unison, "Harry, it is not your time to

be with us. Your place is on Earth.

You are not like those people down there.

You can make a difference in this world,

make it a better place."

Harry felt as if a mountain of fears lifted off his shoulders.

All of a sudden his thoughts were clear and concise.

He looked down at the crowd

and yelled, "Get yourself another sucker."

Carefully he walked toward the open window.

THE LENINGRAD CEMETERY

How peaceful is the cemetery

in Piskaryovskoye, Leningrad.

How beautiful are the blood red roses

tended in perpetual care.

How meaningful is the eternal flame,

a living memorial.

A mass grave for five hundred thousand bodies.

Nine hundred days of struggle

molds heroes and heroines.

Peeling wallpaper to make soup,

some managed to survive.

Bodies heaped one on another

sandwiched in a mass grave.

Their souls yearned in anguish

and pain for a redeemer.

WISHFUL THINKING

Better than toys or peppermint candies,
better than any gift given before,
if I had only one wish you could grant me,
dear Santa, I'd wish you could stop war.

Fill up your sack with brotherly cheer
and bundles of love to last through the year.
Take a giant eraser, wipe out prejudice and hate,
give us all a new heart.
Santa—it would be great.

Give everyone faith in their religion
and don't forget respect of the other.
When this is done, there won't be a need
for brother to fight brother.

Get going Santa, there's work to be done.
Bring peace to the world, to everyone.

<u>THE REVENGE OF OMIE WISE</u>
Written December 19, 1966

They sang the song of Omie Wise,

all throughout the nation.

How she was murdered by a scoundrel.

Poor Omie Wise,

I told her all those lies.

I filled her pretty head

with thoughts of the wedding bed.

Yes, I am Jonathon Lewis

who did poor Omie in.

And now by God I'm suffering,

I'm paying for my sin.

Poor Omie Wise.

a lonely orphan girl.

Gentle and affectionate,

like a kitten she did curl.

She stayed up at the Adams farm

and worked hard for her keep.

She never did defy me,

Omie liked me—quite a heap.

Poor Omie Wise,

her head was full of dreams.

She easily fell prey

to all my ornery schemes.

I knew it was not possible

that she and I could wed,

I wanted not an orphan girl,

but my boss' sister instead.

Poor Omie Wise,

I took her by surprise.

As I plunged my horse in Deep River,

she saw murder in my eyes.

No one dared defy me,

the name Lewis made them quake.

My family's reputation was as

poisonous as a snake.

Poor Omie Wise,

the river folk heard her cries.

They knew murder had been done,

and I was the guilty one.

In Randolph County there was one brave man,

and time did come to pass,

when he came upon me unawares,

as I cuddled a sweet lass.

Poor Omie Wise,

her revenge was doomed to wait.

There was no jail could hold me,

I was living out my fate.

Like as not they would have forgot

about poor Omie Wise,

but for this cussed folk song,

reliving all my lies.

Poor Omie Wise,

have you heard that song?

The story of your plight

will live though you are gone.

I was at a corn shucking near the falls of Ohio,

reminiscing about Deep River and the

hills of Carolina, when this fellow started

singing that darned old song,

all about my awful crime.

Poor Omie Wise,

it came like thunder from the skies.

They're taking me to trial,

and my name they will revile.

I was tried in Guilford County,

and the guards stood near,

with loaded muskets and fixed bayonets.

Many bystanders waited—for the verdict I would get.

Poor Omie Wise,

No witness could tell of your cries.

Either long moved, or passed away,

so I went free that day.

But you saw that justice was done,

Omie Wise, you were the one.

All the way to Kentucky

you came for revenge on me.

Poor Omie Wise,

listen to my plea.

I promise to confess

If you stop haunting me.

But now as I look to the past

at the crime I did commit,

I know I deserve this torment,

the punishment does fit.

PART THREE

ROMANCE WRITINGS

The next section of poetry may fall under the heading
of romance; sometimes serious and elsewhere humorous.
Muriel most enjoyed this subject in television, movies
and books she read.

THE CONVERSATION OF TWO YOUNG LOVERS

"It's going to be fun when we're married.

I'll use the convertible in the summer

and you can have it in the winter," she said.

"Well, I'll just use the station wagon," he replied.

"I'm going to be a blonde, 'cause blondes

 have more fun."

"I'm going to work at the office and come home

later for dinner."

"You better not, the maid goes home at 7pm,

 and it makes her nervous to work overtime.

Let's have four children, two boys and two girls.

I'll put lots of powder on the babies

so they smell nice."

"They have to eat everything on their plate,

or they can't watch television."

"I'm going to all the cocktail parties I'm invited to."

"I'm going to have one night out with the boys

and win lots of money."

"If you lose you won't get any kisses or hugs.

I'm gonna bake you a chocolate cake for

your birthday."

"I'm gonna give you a diamond bracelet for yours,

but I can't invite you to my birthday party

'cause I'll be eight, and this year

I'm only inviting boys."

<u>LA CHAISE LOUNGE AU JARDIN</u>

She sits on the plastic chaise

while oleander and cypress

stand guard greenly in the perfumed garden.

Her book lies open on her lap

as her lover, the sun

splatters her eyes,

lingers on her milk white skin

and turns her into a splotched lobster

as she dreams of kaleidoscopes.

<u>DOUBLE OR NOTHING</u>

There is much that can be said

for the old-fashioned double bed.

If you and hubby have a fight

you can steal back in the night.

Listen to your heart, not head,

use a French perfume instead.

Cuddle up close and snuggle tight

topple your king, play it right.

Dump all those how-to books you've read.

Get yourself a double bed.

THREE LITTLE WORDS

Three little words

I LOVE YOU

can steal a heart

that's been broken

in two.

Three little words

I LOVE YOU

can change how you feel

and the things that

you do.

Three little words

I LOVE YOU

open the windows

of your soul

to a bright sunny view.

THE ELIGIBLE MALE

Oh what fools we women be

playing the game of matrimony.

Before the marriage we do research

on how to get him into the church.

We hunt our mate with cunning skill,

big game hunters on the kill.

We consult the hip news,

we follow the stars.

He couldn't escape

if he went to Mars.

We play it hot.

We play it cool.

We make exceptions

to the rule.

If any female stands in our way,

we break all rules of decent fair play.

We are secret agents

searching to find

that eligible male

and brainwash his mind.

The die is cast,

he caught the bait.

The fish is hooked.

He cannot wait.

Up to the altar,

on with the ring.

Take all the vows,

promise anything.

The ceremony is ended.

You're ready to go

into the marriage inferno.

HAPPY VALENTINE'S DAY

You are my own sweet valentine

nestled deep within my heart.

You are the goodness and the wisdom

that emerges to face the darkness

and make it light.

I am so lucky to have you as my valentine.

You bring me strength and happiness.

If you will be my valentine

I'll be yours, and together

we will bring joy into each

other's life.

WHATEVER YOU DO

Whatever you do

don't take me for granted.

I will give you my love freely,

but no contract

will make me your slave.

I am my own person,

I will move as the mood strikes me.

My love must flow motivated by

tenderness and appreciation.

Don't take me for granted,

or I will harden my heart.

My flesh will be cold and stiff,

instead of soft and yielding.

My kiss a frosty winter morn,

no longer a hot summer night.

WHEN THE FULL MOON APPEARS

1982 WAS THE YEAR OF THE BEARD FOR ME.

FORMERLY FINDING HAIRY MEN REPULSIVE, RE-
PUGNANT, RAPACIOUS.

I WANTED BLACKBEARD ON ONE ARM
AND RED BEARD ON THE OTHER.

CLEAN SHAVEN MEN WERE BILLIARD
BALLS, LACKLUSTER LILLIES,
NINCOMPOOPS, SILLIES.

LUCKILY FOR ME NOBODY GOT MY MESSAGE!

THE SEDUCTION

You planned the seduction, sly minx,

every detail finely honed,

every motion subtle and measured.

Under a blanket of stars,

in a basin used for ablution

an oil lamp your spotlight.

You took that bath, Bathsheba.

The splash that made history.

You could have turned away, David,

sang a psalm of protection,

asked the Lord for guidance.

When she let down her hair,

black as a raven's wing.

Her body white as alabaster.

She was singing in your flesh,

drowning out the sound of safety.

PART FOUR

WRITINGS OF THE CREATIVE PROCESS

Muriel was very concerned with the creative process in the art of writing.

LITTLE POEM

"Bring me a little poem," she said.

Gathering a bouquet of thoughts

pragmatic, playful, tied together

with trivia, and the reddest of ribbon.

I put them inside a wooden bucket

and lowered them into a well.

The small mother-of-pearl bead

placed in the oyster, kept in sheltered bays.

It layers itself like an onion becoming

a perfect pearl, a unique rainbow.

I want to string together

a jeweled necklace of iridescent words.

A treasure of incubation and final emergence,

that sings a siren song linking you to me.

"A little poem is easier said than done," I say.

ADVICE FOR THE BUDDING POET

Linger where the literary gather.

Pick up a tidbit, or a smatter.

Read the experts, study the news.

Seek inspiration, invoke the Muse.

Meditate, go into a trance.

Jump the waves, hear the words dance.

Get it out of the dark where it languishes and lingers.

Type, mail with SASE and cross your fingers.

POET'S DILEMMA

I'm a hero, seeing a mission

with no place to go.

My beautiful voices have deserted me

and I am on my own.

Yet they seem to linger in the background,

silent and unobtrusive watching the comedy.

Which to my own muted brain

is becoming tragic indeed.

Ah, how exquisite a torture,

to play on an unsuspecting victim.

To be awaked, aroused and desirous

of playing the game.

Only to find I am the sole participant.

The strategy has already unfolded

and I am caught in the middle.

The challenge is still provocative,

but half empty like a vessel only partially

filled, yet craving to spill over.

POEMS FOR SALE

I don't know iambic pentameter

so my meter may be off key.

I don't know simile from salami,

but that's okay with me.

My metaphors seem to mix and match.

My images seem to hold and catch.

I've got a geyser in my head

that's boiling and spouting,

so I am shouting POEMS, POEMS, POEMS.

I'm selling —are you buying, Mister, huh?

LATCHING ON

Drifting along

aimlessly, aimlessly

to and fro

till I latch on to something

a lifeline

the poem begins.

A PRAYER FOR SLEEP

Listen to the plea of
your poor bedraggled servant.

Hear my plea, I entreat You
and beg You to heal me.

Bring me back to my old self,
bring me back to health.

I am at wit's end.
Please, please a healing.

Bring me rest.
Your gift of sleep.
A thousandfold I will thank You.

POET'S LAMENT

I don't want to ever hear again

that poetry does not pay.

Even though I know it's the truth

it really ruins my day.

If the public only knew how poets

suffer and toil.

To create the perfect poem

we burn the midnight oil.

A poem is a thing of beauty

crafted with care.

Do you think the public appreciates,

they read and stare.

So like the turtle who won the race,

our skins are very tough.

In order to be a true poet my friend,

persevere and know your stuff.

LOST AND FOUND

God is a no-no in Poetry 210.

I'm giving you fair warning my friend.

If you've traveled the celestial trail beware.

If the light burns brightly in your spine,

put on the dimmer.

I've seen young men with bulging biceps

blanch at the sound of His name.

Any Tuesday or Thursday between 1:30 and 3:00

you can see God and Darwin running

the 100-yard dash.

Darwin usually wins.

But there is a faint glimmer gleaning

through the blurred original papers

passed from hand to hand.

Somewhere God can be found

in the eternal flutter.

RIGHT BRAIN VS. LEFT BRAIN

My right brain is fighting my left brain.

They're into a bit of a tiff.

Intuition vs. logic.

Is it yes, no or if?

My left brain is very pragmatic.

My right brain can wax ecstatic.

Left brain gets the answer digging down deep.

Right brain gets the answer in dreams asleep.

The battle between the brains will

be beguiling for ages.

It will be the topic of discussion

among professors and sages.

If the left brain doesn't know what the right brain is doing,

then a constant battle is forever ensuing.

Have a friendly meeting of the mind,

let right and left brain seek and find.

The inevitable outcome will probably

be a no-win situation, because each

brain says "ME."

AMAZING MUSE

Have you ever stopped to ponder

where are the Muses out yonder?

Are they all descendants of the ancient Greek,

but just think of all the languages they speak.

Perhaps they are kin to the wandering Jews

who gave us the Bible with bad and good news.

Did your Muse say Eureka when it did arrive

and feed you manna to help you survive?

Does the Muse pick people out of a hat

like a Chinese menu, one of this and one of that?

Do the comics have an amusing Muse

who spits out jokes that just can't lose?

Do they throw in extra atoms for the physicists to

make the breakthrough without computers and lists?

Do they give the composer music and lyrics too,

and the fire to inspire a very special few?

And the gift to the novelist of all those words

that come racing along in thundering herds?

And the inventor sitting at his desk at night

in a moment of repose does he see the light?

Is it one Muse or many, and how do you get one?

There aren't any how-to-books on how it's done.

I guess a Muse picks and chooses winners and losers,

and can determine the teetotalers and the boozers.

Maybe if I meditate, pray and eat the right foods

in the middle of the night I might find me a Muse.

PART FIVE

FRIENDSHIP WRITINGS

If Muriel did not spend a day of her life not in the company of one or more friends then I would give you a dollar for any of those days. She loved people and therefore people loved Muriel. One of her favorite songs was "People Who Need People" sung by Barbra Streisand. Below please find below some things she had to say about her friends. Muriel often pleased her friends by giving a little poem written about them.

<u>A FRIEND</u>

A friend is one of those hidden treasures

whose worth and value is hard to measure.

You don't have to see them everyday,

but you know they are there in a special way.

You only have to pick up the phone

and they make you feel not alone.

In happiness and in times of sorrow

a friend sticks by you today and tomorrow.

Thank you for your friendship

thru happiness and strife.

<u>TRIBUTE TO GISELLA</u>

GISELLA COMPUTER ANGEL

GISELLA HEALING AGENT

GISELLA MARRIAGE MINISTER ANGEL

GISELLA BELLY DANCER ANGEL

GISELLA TAX EXPERT ANGEL

GISELLA FRIEND ANGEL

GISELLA YOU ARE MULTIFACETED

GISELLA EXTRAORDINAIRE

GISELLA YOU'RE THE TOPS

GISELLA stop blushing, it's un-angelic.

<u>A FRANKFUL DAY</u>

Frank was the best friend and buddy of Muriel's husband George.

A FRANKLESS DAY

George eats sour cream and cottage cheese for lunch.

A FRANKFUL DAY

George and Frank eat out Chinese, Vietnamese or fish.

A FRANKLESS DAY

George is gloomy, a lost soul.

A FRANKFUL DAY

George is lively, in good humor, achieves his goals.

So here's to more days that are Frankful,

less lunches to prepare

and for that I am thankful.

GIOVANNI ITALIAN RESTAURANT

A favorite place to eat, visited regularly by Muriel and George.
Their favorite waiters were identical triplets.

We are the triplets three

who work with Giovanni.

Our mother named us Jeff, Joe, and James,

to make her proud of her are our aims.

We always dress in formal attire

and serve you what is your heart's desire.

We're most sincere and use the utmost discretion,

trust us, we won't betray your confession.

We pamper all our customers who we adore,

to make sure they come back to us for more.

In our tux we may look silly or glitzy,

but we're really sincere.

We'll take a stand on issues, just lend us your ear.

To identify us can be confusing,

but just remember our names.

We are the famous triplets from Giovanni,

Jeff, Joe and James.

WHAT MAKES AN EMILY ?
*Emily was an artist and friend who did drawings
for Muriel's very first book about animal rhymes.*

What makes an Emily?

What secret potion

carouses within

emitting signals of love,

evoking cosmic harmony.

What makes an Emily?

Temper sod buried,

ready to root

at provocation.

Red is for rage—isn't it?

What makes an Emily?

Gardens of sun kissed

wildflowers—potpourri

of God's magic,

locus of humanity.

<u>JENNIFER</u>
Jennifer gave Muriel bridge lessons.

Have you ever met a Jennifer?

Best meet her on a rainy day,

or when you're feeling down.

Suddenly the sun comes shining through

the steely gray clouds.

A Roman candle rainbow sputters

across the sky.

I don't know why.

She is beautiful within,

and her bones will not turn to plastic.

She makes the old feel young,

and the young feel wise.

She is crowned with beauty.

Her hair is wild and free, as is her heart.

Her eyes are butterfly wings.

Her mouth is a little girl's—and yet a woman.

Her body moves like the gentle flowing river.

She is peace she is Jennifer.

Why am I crying?

Why do the tears flow and drop on my sleeve

like a pear-shaped diamond?

I cry because my inner voices show me beauty

and the joy is too painful to bear.

Muriel lived the last decade of her life at Abbotswood, an
independent living facility in Greensboro. Every evening
for years, she sat at the same table for dinner with a
group of ladies who became her close friends.
She wrote about these and other friends in Abbotswood.

<u>HAPPY BIRTHDAY ANITA</u>

Nothing could be sweeter

than to be with Anita,

Happy Birthday.

We wish they allowed seven

at the dinner table,

but at Abbotswood rules are six.

Anita, if you don't mind,

we can fit you into the mix.

Anita we know you were a bowler big time,

so bowl us over Anita, that suits us just fine.

HAPPY BIRTHDAY GOLDIE

Goldie your hair matches your name.

Gold, bouffant and beautiful.

Goldie your smile matches your name.

It says, I'll be your friend.

You are a friend loyal and true,

may you have good health in whatever you do.

HAPPY BIRTHDAY HALINA

Happy birthday dear Halina.

You keep our spirits high

with jokes and a song every night.

Halina —92 is only a number

and everyday you get younger.

So relax and enjoy your birthday

with love and kisses from your pals

who sit with you at dinner,

the Abbotswood gals.

HAPPY BIRTHDAY JOAN

We the invincible six pay tribute

to our dear friend Joan.

94 is only a number and

no one would guess your age.

You are such a classy lady

and as brave as Joan of Arc.

Joan you are compassionate

loving, warm and very smart.

You are the greatest hugger

and I crown you Queen of the Arts.

<u>HAPPY BIRTHDAY ILLIEN</u>

Illien, you've reached the big 90.

Why not join the 90 and over club?

The nineties can be exciting and

revealing if you just forget your woes.

This is how it goes:

If someone asks, "How are you feeling?"

Say GREAT! Even if it is a white lie.

If you think positive thoughts

you will believe without knowing why.

We're here to celebrate with you

and love you, and make a big fuss.

So welcome to the nineties Illien,

the party is on us!

<u>HAPPY BIRTHDAY TO ME</u>

I'm 92, boo hoo, boo hoo.

Wishing I could turn 92 back to 29.

But today is my birthday and I'm feeling fine.

I don't care if the March winds blow,

but on my birthday, please no snow.

I'm enthralled by my pals at dinner,

they're cheerful and each is a winner.

My life is lively and lovely at Abbotswood.

I wish myself health, happiness and everything good.

PART SIX

HUMOROUS WRITINGS

*Uplifting people through writing funny poetry
was an exciting challenge that Muriel enjoyed.*

I WANTUM SOME QUANTUM

*Werner Heisenberg (1901-1976) a German physicist, was
among the first to expound a theory of quantum mechanics.*

I wantum some quantum,

some quantum I wantum.

Mr. Heisenberg, if you please.

I'm confused, perplexed,

dumbfounded and hexed.

You will soon have me climbing up trees.

I've a penchant for piecing together

the puzzle that was blasted with the big bang.

I'd like to walk upon the moon.

If only I'd get the hang.

I'm desperately in need of a charge,

and I don't mean Master or Visa.

I need an atom or Adam

that I can hugga and squeeza.

I wantum some quantum, some quantum I wantum.

<u>MY KIND OF GAME—-MAHJONG</u>
Muriel wrote this for her group of women
who regularly played Mahjong.

Confucius says, "If you play mahjong

you will be happy, not forlorn."

It's the game of chance

more fun than romance.

Woman and man take heed,

with mahjong you can succeed.

You will exercise your mind

using tiles that you will find.

If Confucius tells you so,

mahjong is the way to go.

<u>IN ORDER TO BE HEALTY, WEALTHY & WISE</u>

Muriel always talked about needing to lose some
weight, going to work out, and getting more healthy.
The key here is she always talked about that, but I don't remember
her doing much about it.

Drink eight glasses of water—I'll tell you why.

Your skin will be supple, not wrinkled or dry.

Don't gulp, drink slowly, let your imagination soar.

You're on a beach chair listening to the ocean's roar.

You have to get a new attitude.

You really have to get in the mood.

So drink up—here's a toast to you new life.

May you be healthy, happy, and never have strife.

Drink eight glasses of water a day.

I don't like to drink water, I'll say.

Rethink, re-evaluate this sage recommendation.

Water is the staff of life, not deserving condemnation.

Think of all the pills you ingest every day,

with only a few sips of water, you'll say Oy Vey.

DON'T CALL ME AN OLD BAG
"Hermes son of Zeus and Maia, messenger of the gods."

I am a Hermes bag,

like the gods I am eternal.

I am valued by rich society women

and envied by many a working girl.

My skin is supple and never wrinkles.

My accessory parts are memorable, original, one of a kind.

I reside at the most exclusive high fashion shops.

I am often displayed in the window accompanying

a memorable dress, suit or other piece of clothing.

I have appeared in advertisements of international

haute couture magazines with beautiful models,

but I am always the main attraction.

Working girls save their money for years

so we can possess me.

I heard that in Tokyo a young secretary slept

with me in bed after the boyfriend left her.

If someone tires of me, I can be sold at an exclusive

vintage shop, but the price is always in the high brackets.

I am never discarded,

if you desire me please check me out.

I am worth it!

WHAT DR. SPOCK NEVER TAUGHT

Mother don't baby your boy

cut the umbilical cord.

He wants to grow up macho

become Chairman of the Board.

He needs his independence

to be strong, autonomous,

but he can't seem to sever

attachment to the mom-in-us.

When he brings his intended

to show to the family

you might find a resemblance

to the girl you used to be.

Teach your boy household chores

to treat women as his equal.

You'll be mother-in-law supreme

and his marriage won't have a sequel.

THE SANTA CLAUS BLUES

"Santa, Santa

why are you moping?

The reindeer are ready,

the children are hoping

to have a fine Christmas

full of good cheer.

At the rate you're going

you'll never get there."

"Mrs. Claus, Mrs. Claus

this world is a mess.

I can't take the pressure

I must confess.

I don't get respect

children pull at my beard.

They question my existence

they think I am weird."

"Papa Claus you've been
watching too much TV.
Don't believe everything
you hear and see."

"Video games and computers
make my head whirl and buzz.
Oh, my aching back—
I ain't this way I was."

"Santa, what you need
is a dose of good cheer.
Remember you're loved
by the children out there.
You need to relax
and become more tranquil.
Here's a Valium dear Santa.
Go—and be thankful."

THE SWEET SMELL OF SUCCESS

They say chicken soup is therapeutic,

good for what ails you when you are sick.

But when the chicken is cooking in the pot,

on the savory smell I become a drunken sot.

The odor of carrots, onions, and celery,

can anything smell better—someone please tell me.

It's better than incense or a French perfume.

It may even enable you to catch a groom.

So ask Momma or Bubbe for the recipe.

If you say 'pretty please' you can even ask me.

PART SEVEN

JUDAIC WRITINGS

Muriel participated actively in the Beth David Synagogue as a volunteer and leader in committees, projects, and event planning. She also wrote pieces that had to do with her Jewish faith.

GREETING THE SABBATH QUEEN

There aromatic smell of chicken soup

and pot roast assault my senses.

Daily newspapers are spread

over shiny wooden like linoleum.

I pick them up before dinner,

read the screaming headlines.

Our home radiates festivity,

sparkling china, polished silver,

a white linen tablecloth.

The braided challah

glazed to perfection,

rests royally under

an embroidered covering.

The kiddish cup, filled with wine,

the brass candlestick awaits

the lighting, the blessing.

Momma's golden hair

is braided into a crown.

Over her special Friday night dress

she wears a crocheted apron.

When I hug her she feels

as soft as my down pillow.

SHIVA CALL
*Shiva is the Jewish period of mourning for
the passing of a loved one.*

May God comfort you and bring you peace.

May life's sorrow and anguish cease.

May sweet memories of a loved one past

surround you and hold you fast.

No jokes, no small talk, just this phrase.

May friends and relatives who pay a shiva call

lift up your spirits, not let you fall.

May God comfort you in all His wondrous way.

SUKKOT DINNER UNDER THE STARS

Muriel became fast friends with the new Chabad House
established in Greensboro.

At the Sukkot dinner under the stars

the kiddush and candle lighting ceremony

made your heart sing.

Hindy cooked stuffed cabbage, chicken salad,

butternut squash and a rice medley.

This was a royal meal fit for a King.

Rabbi Plotkin shared jokes and wise words from Torah.

Everyone enjoyed the friendship

and warmth of this special holiday night.

At the Sukkot dinner under the stars

mitzvahs embraced us all in awe and wonder.

Together we basked in the heavenly light.

ONE PEOPLE ONE DESTINY

This poem was dedicated to all the people who participated with Muriel on a United Jewish Appeal trip to Israel.

This land, holy of holies, haven for the homeless,

this State of Israel, small in size,

but a giant in spirit, has captured our hearts,

fired our imaginations.

As she takes us unto her bosom

we feel her agonies, her anguish,

and the pride of her many accomplishments.

We have trod her soil, studied her history,

realized her ambitions, her fears,

and walked in the footsteps of her heroes.

We take back to America memories

of a shared experience of laughter and tears,

and the knowledge born anew that we are one,

and though we cannot complete the task

we must persevere, and with God's help

make the dream a reality.

<u>MY ANGEL MENACHEM</u>
Muriel met the Rebbe Menachem Schneerson, leader of the Chabad movement and kept a photo of him on her nightstand.

M..........MEMORY

E...........ENERGY

N..........NESHOMAH

A...........ANGEL

CH........CHABAD

E...........EXAMPLE

M.........MIRACLES

FESTIVAL OF LIGHTS

Chanukah lights shine,

shine your glory on me,

forge molten memories

of history past,

Judah and his tiny band

of Maccabees.

Menorah lights blaze,

eight nights of remembrance.

Remember the tyrant Antiochus,

and how justice triumphed

over iniquity.

Candelabra glow,

kindle the candles bright.

Relive the miracle of Chanukah,

this 25th day of Kislev.

Fill the world with light.

<u>START WITH YOURSELF</u>
Inspired by the scholar and Rabbi Adin Steinsaltz.

Start with yourself, do it today.

Pick up the Bible, it has much to say.

This ancient text

continues to shine.

Perhaps because

its words are divine.

And if you get a hint

or a glimmer,

dive into its depths

and become a swimmer.

Start with yourself

the world will be bright.

Your life won't be humdrum,

but infused with light.

You will be an example

for all to see.

You will be living continuity.

POWER OF PRAYER

*During his sixties, Muriel's husband George was in and
out of hospitals undergoing numerous major operations.*

When I was awakened

and the dream was still going on,

I knew it was for real.

When I leaned over

to pat the cold empty bed sheet,

I knew it was real.

Then the decision

to fight the enemy

with Light blasted the stillness.

Brothers and sisters

in your churches and synagogues

light the candles,

say prayers of healing.

Circles of healing

from the far corners of the Earth.

Today the knife cuts,

but the pure circle of His Light

will protect and heal.

I know, for it is real.

LEND AN EAR, JOHN LOCKE

*In 1668, John Locke composed the Fundamental
Constitution of the Carolinas, in which it was expressly
stated that the colony was to be open to settlement by
"Jews, heathens and other dissenters" and any seven or
more persons agreeing in any religion should constitute
a church or profession.*— Encyclopedia Judaica, Vol. 12
*This part of the history of North Carolina Judaism is
the focus of the next poem.*

John Locke, into one huge pot

you dropped Jews, heathens, dissenters;

odd ingredients for a North Carolina stew.

Jews wove a mystic seven into the Bible's fabric.

Heathens worshiped five planets, sun and moon.

Do you remember proclaiming:

"Revolution in some circumstances is

not only a right, but an obligation."

Jewish volunteers marched in Washington's Army

In the 40th Infantry six Cohen brothers wore grey.

Your words: "Each man has a right

to the product of his labor."

Later immigrants peddled pots and pans.

"Egg-eaters", the Cherokee called Jews

who stocked their meat at way stations.

You believed: The mind is born blank,

a tabula rasa upon which the world describes itself.

Jews fought and bled for state and country.

The Cones of Greensboro wove textile dynasties

and patterned welfare programs.

In blue ink, Jewish merchants, lawmakers, benefactors

wrote their history on North Carolina pages.

Well done, John Locke!

PART EIGHT

NATURE & ENVIRONMENTAL WRITINGS

I remember as a child my mother driving me and talking about how beautiful the nature around us looked. That made an impression on me as it was the first time my awareness was turned to this subject which I took for granted.

A LOVE FOR ALL SEASONS

I want to believe in fairy tales.

That a note in a bottle can travel to Wales.

I want to believe wishes can come true

to those who wish hard enough…me and you.

I want to believe we can love one another,

despite our color, we are sister and brother.

I want to believe in a spirit that is free

and allows us individual identity.

I want to believe love is for all seasons

not special holidays or special reasons.

Let us all be givers and not receivers.

Together we can be beloved believers.

THE ARBORETUM

***A favorite place for Muriel to spend time was at
the Arboretum grounds in Greensboro.***

I walked in the Arboretum

lush with bloom and greenery

and I said, "God, wherefore art Thou?"

I felt a soft breeze

and a stirring in the trees

and I said, "God is in the breeze

and the trees."

Later I saw a stream

gently rippling over stones,

and I said, "God is in the

rippling stream."

But still I said, "God, wherefore art Thou?"

I heard a voice say, "Look into your heart."

Then a soft whispering: "Here am I"

and I knew God had shown me His way.

And it was good.

THE OLD MILL

There used to be an old attractive abandoned mill near the school which my sisters, brother and I attended.

Lonely, lonely stands the mill

all alone and quite forsaken.

Swiftly, swiftly runs the brook.

Time is running, running swiftly.

Soon your waters will be stilled.

Running only through my mind.

Brace yourself old mill.

Here comes the mighty bulldozer.

To run you down into the ground

and scatter you far and wide.

One day concrete will cover you.

Rolling wheels will sing to you.

Who will remember your weathered stone?

Who will recall the brook so cool?

Who can say you can't stop progress?

Only fools like me.

THE MORNING AFTER THE STORM

Greensboro usually has mild winters with an early spring.
If there is snow it is gone in a day or two at the most.

At first glance a sigh escaped my lips,

at the exquisite beauty of it all.

A gigantic set for a Hollywood extravaganza on ice?

No! Saturday morning after the ice storm.

Greensboro, N.C.—February 18th, 1967

The ice glistened on the trees,

and they collectively became appendages

of an enormous crystal chandelier,

their prisms sparkling rainbows,

as the sun gaily cavorted from limb to limb.

But then, as my eye drifted downward,

to my horror and surprise,

there appeared first one tree,

then another, and yet another,

all bent over in most grotesque positions,

as if they were playing

a macabre game of freeze tag.

And lying on the ground were the victims

of the storm, maimed and dead.

Nevermore to know the beauty of spring,

the injured patiently waited for help,

that might never come,

baring to the world their gaping wounds.

But already the sun was melting the chains of ice

and the survivors began straining to rise up again,

and give thanks to God.

THE PEAKS OF OTTER

*The Peaks of Otter are three mountain peaks in the Blue
Ridge Mountains overlooking the town of Bedford, Virginia.*

Oh, those Peaks of Otter,

on an autumn day.

What magnificence and glory

in their fall display.

Stretching as far,

as the eye can see,

in myriad shapes of fantasy.

The autumn wind nestles,

up to the trees,

while the shifting sun,

plays games with the leaves.

Till like a chameleon,

the colors do confuse,

in a glorious maze

of autumn hues.

If only I could paint this scene,

beautiful beyond my widest dream,

but the master painter did this for me,

in His open air gallery.

So all you doubting Thomases,

who question if God is dead,

take yourself to the Peaks of Otter,

and find the truth instead.

Take you there on an autumn day,

and open up your eyes.

Drink in the wonder and glory,

let your spirits soar to the skies.

ACID RAIN IN NORTH CAROLINA'S MOUNTAINS

***The Eternal God took man (Adam) and placed him in the
Garden of Eden, to keep it and watch over it. (Genesis 2:15)***

The trees hover above.

Their Holocaust has come.

Stunted, stripped of bark and greenery,

branches lopsided, broken,

their exposed frames cry "Help".

It is spring, but there is no renewal,

no green awakening, only skeletons

and seasons that run together.

The wind and clouds know,

made accomplices to the crime.

On their backs flew

the devils of destruction

spitting sulfur dioxide

from power plants and factories

in Tennessee and Ohio

targeting our highest trees.

In fields of loneliness,

a landscape of broken dreams,

the trees shamefully cry out

to God and man in a chorus

of repentance and pleas for redemption

"a healing, a healing, please, a healing."

THE MAY SKY

How glorious the sky on a day in May,

just before God pulls down the curtain

and we are surrounded

by the black of darkness.

It's as if your time is numbered

and in just a few minutes

the vast panorama of nature will vanish.

So goodbye to brilliant rosy hues

and intricate shadings of blue

with fleecy white clouds

ba-ba-ba-ing their way to sleep.

THE WAYS OF SPRING

*Muriel's children were influenced by the sixties
and seventies, and she watched with great interest.*

When Spring arriveth,

Milady deriveth much pleasure,

stepping forth in her finery for its welcome.

No matter how blustery the wind bloweth,

Milady knoweth.

Venture forth she must, the world is waiting.

And across the nation,

girl watchers man their stations,

the better to stretch the eye,

as the miniskirt rides to the sky,

young and fancy free.

And mod young things angelic,

in colors psychedelic,

flirt with unrestrained passion,

with Dame Fashion.

Spring is the season

for young and for old,

when the heart is warmed

from the Winter's cold.

Spring is the tonic,

that Nature brings.

Spring is Spring,

is Spring, is Spring.

PART NINE

SOMETHING ABOUT ME

Speaking about herself, Muriel reveals some interesting insights, interests and experiences in the following writings.

<u>W.H. AUDEN WHEREVER YOU ARE</u>

A true whimsical story includes the famous writer W.H. Auden.

1. I didn't send for you W.H.

but somebody was trying to put us together.

It all started with the *Today Show*

in of all places,

between my bedroom and the den.

Like a bolt out of the blue

your deep resonant voice

entered my consciousness

for the first time,

and in a telepathic flash

the name AUDEN.

And this was the beginning.

2. George has an ambidextrous mind

so it was easy for him

to read the morning paper

and still watch the *Today Show.*

"George, is that Auden?"

"Yes dear," he answered.

If I told George

the Messiah is coming,

he would say:

"Yes dear, please pass the sugar."

3. I cornered Dr. Taylor after class.
(*He of the burning eyes and a Rasputin look which had
taught me that openness is the gateway to perception.*)

"Dr. Taylor, could this have been mental telepathy?"

"Absolutely not."

4. I read in the paper, W.H., that you

were going back to Oxford, and

on the spur of the moment

I decided to call him.

Something really strange happened.

I asked for New York Information

and was immediately put through

without the mandatory 1-212-555-1212.

"Can I help you?

"Yes, please connect me with W.H. Auden.

Greenwich Village, Manhattan.

5. A few seconds, a phone ringing

and your voice.

"Hello."

"Mr. Auden, I want to wish you a happy Easter."

"What a lovely thing to do."

And then I froze and all I could say was, "Goodbye."

6. Sorry you didn't make poet laureate,

but if it's any consolation

you were written up in my *World Book*

as Foremost Poet of his Generation.

So long W.H., see you in my dreams.

THE BATTLE OF THE BODY STATS

George sets the thermostat at 69

I prefer 70…that suits me fine.

One degree below my eyes tear,

my nose runs, allergies I fear.

I gulp antihistamine, aspirin too,

make a prayer, "Please God, no flu,"

and climb into bed with ten frigid toes,

two slabs of ice arms, a cherry-freeze nose.

With pity George rubs me and blows down my back

to give me the extra heat I lack.

Life could be so heavenly

if George would give me one degree.

WHAT'S MY NAME?
Muriel would often write things she heard
after being awakened in the middle of the night.

Anne called me Miriam three times.

This was very unusual, my name is Muriel.

If I had done it I could understand, but her—

never in a million years.

She with her PhD in Greek literature.

A real brain.

Besides, this was my second term in Poetry 210,

and she was also in my Writers Club.

When she called me Miriam the first time

I said, "It's Muriel."

Within a few seconds she said Miriam again

and I said, "It's Muriel."

And after a few more minutes Anne said again,

Miriam, and people in the class said, "Muriel."

My mother could not make up her mind

about my name and gave me three names—

Marcella, Caroline and finally ended up

naming me after a cigar "Muriel."

Mother is also named after a cigar, "Henrietta."

So when Anne, the high priestess of poetry, gives

me the name Miriam I guess I should be honored.

After all Miriam was the sister of Moses

and a prophetess in her own right.

When it happened I didn't give it a second thought,

but riding home in the car I thought it was peculiar.

It was so unusual as to arouse my Cabalistic curiosity.

It had happened right after Anne had told the class,

"Twenty-five years ago, if a poem were written

about a talking tree community, it would have

been with God and not with the wind."

I put in my two cents and said, "Trees don't talk

to God, people do."

Anne replied, "Miriam talks to God and He answers back."
And I said, "He talks with me, but He doesn't spell."

This was an inside joke because one of those
special messages I received in the middle of the
night contained the word 'anoint', and I had the
hardest time finding the spelling for this word.

I also found the word in the *Greensboro Daily News*
in an article announcing the anointment of
Fred Chapell as Professor of English.

But to get back to my new name Miriam,
I began to wonder about Anne's health.
She was in a wheelchair recovering from a back injury,
and she said one leg felt warmer than the other.
She had been taking codeine.
Could she have spoken from an altered state
of consciousness?

I couldn't have been that curious, because that

was on Thursday, and it wasn't till Sunday that

I began to think about it again.

This time I decided to look up Miriam in

the *Book of Jewish Knowledge*.

I had that funny feeling in the pit of my stomach

that I usually have when something is going to happen—

something mystical.

This was the quote: "And they, in turn, taking fire

from him (Moses) sang with him.

Also Miriam the prophetess, the sister of

Aaron, took a timbrel in her hand, and all the

women went out after her with timbrels and danced.

Miriam too sang the Song of Moses:

Sing ye to the Lord, for He is highly exalted.

The horse and his rider hath He thrown into the sea."

Then all of a sudden like a thunderbolt I remembered

I had written something in a similar vein when

I had been in Raleigh at a branch board meeting

in the beginning of October.

I hadn't even typed it up yet.

It was still scribbled on that piece of paper.

We were assigned to thought

groups about the Jewish holidays.

My holiday was Shavuot which celebrated the giving of

the Ten Commandment to Moses.

That night I was awakened by these words:

Come ye upon My mountain and we will sing

and dance and give blessings to the Lord.

The settings were different.

Miriam's was the Red Sea and mine was the mountain.

I take it to be Mt. Sinai, but they both refer to song and

dance, and giving blessings to the Lord.

MY ENERGY

It's conclusive my energy is elusive.

It is here when the sun shows her face.

But when the barometer falls it stalls.

My get up and go loses its pace.

I want my energy to be perky

enable me to go out on the town,

but I can't shop till I drop.

Like a wet mop, my energy goes down, down, down.

Is it the allergies or the air

that triggers this sudden malaise?

My energy has a mind of its own.

and always seems to be in a new phase.

I've tried vitamins and energy drinks,

but they're a temporary shot in the arm.

I admit I can't get my energy back,

and all I can say is darn, darn, darn.

THE VISION ON MY BEDROOM WALL

Gazing into the crystal ball

the fortune teller said:

"In another lifetime your were a famous poet.

I see violent death at a young age—drowning."

I rubbed my eyes. Illusion, hallucination?

That face staring, piercing eyes,

sensuous lips, and dark wavy hair.

The names Keats, Shelley,

commandeered my brain.

Through the partially opened bathroom

door, George lathered up.

When I return my gaze to the bedroom wall

the vision vanished.

Heart pounding I opened my *World Book.*

Keats—no. Shelley it is you!

Cause of death—drowning!

Shelley somewhere you said you

wanted to return as a prophet.

Those words you interrupted my sleep with last night:

"How beateth thou wild wild heart?"

Would surely die a violent death

drowning in an editor's wastebasket.

Shelley dear, put your lips to the

West wind. Speak to me, speak to me.

MEETING UP WITH JESUS ON THE ROAD

Muriel claims to have seen Jesus three times on a ride
to Charlotte. Each time it happened when passing a church.

Riding down to Charlotte, reading Rabbi Abraham Heschel.

For the third time I saw Jesus.

JESUS

Standing from the churchyard to the steeple,

brown-eyed,

bearded,

white robed,

sandaled,

arms outstretched,

inviting,

entreating.

What does Jesus want

with a nice Jewish girl like me?

Then I remembered that he

was a nice Jewish boy.

MEETING UP WITH JESUS ON THE ROAD

STONES AND BONES

Mick Jagger, were we destined to meet

in a mystical manner, extremely offbeat?

Two incidents completely unrelated in time,

each uniquely different in rhythm and rhyme.

The first precipitated by a kidney stone,

I was in a hospital room, afraid and alone.

Turned on the TV to the *Ed Sullivan Show*

and there were The Rolling Stones raring to go.

I danced to their beat a fast Lindy Hop,

went to the bathroom, the stone did drop.

Several decades later I was having fun;

didn't know my troubles had just begun.

Imitating Mick Jagger doing air guitar,

I jumped, turned my ankle, gone too far.

Fell on my wrist and broke the bone.

I'm in a plaster cast with time to atone.

I've had my revelation and my satisfaction.

I am now content to let Mick do all the action.

HAS ANYONE SEEN MY AURA?

I was sitting by the pool at the Hilton
when this psychic came up to me.
"You have the prettiest white aura,
it's been my good fortune to see."

Unaccustomed to psychic phenomenon,
I was befuddled, bedazzled, and dazed.
But before you could holler Kabbalah,
I was off on my journey into space.

I hopped a plane to my daughter's digs
down south in Atlanta.
On the floor with some long-haired hippies
sat my daughter Ellen meditating away.

While surveying this strange sight
a young man saddled up close to me.

"Ma'am you sure have the prettiest white aura

it's been my good fortune to see."

Mirror, mirror on the wall, do I have

the prettiest white aura of all?

If it is true perchance, how can it be

obvious to strangers, yet hidden from me.

PART TEN

INSPIRATION & ENCOURAGEMENT

Muriel seemed to always have a positive attitude; never critical, confrontational or mean spirited. She liked to give encouragement, and the following writings reflect this.

COURAGE: part 1 and part 2

Have courage in yourself.

Whatever you want can be.

Say: "I'll do what I set my mind to.

I am I. I will do…and be."

Have courage my friend.

Fight your battle with renewed vigor,

strength of character, determination,

and if pain persists bear it as a temporary burden.

A stepping stone on the way to recovery,

for though the path is long and weary

have courage my friend,

remember you do not walk alone.

<u>FIREWORKS</u>

Suddenly the sky opened, and the fireworks
came tumbling down.
I started to run, but wherever I ran
they followed me, fiery dragons,
breathing red, orange and blue flames,
down my back.

I could run no more, and throwing myself down
on the cool damp grass,
I listened to the clock in my chest.

Then a strong pair of arms lifted me
high and held me close.
A soft voice whispered,
"Don't be afraid, my darling, you're safe now."
I looked up, and stars were shining in my Mother's eyes.

TRY A LITTLE KINDNESS

Try a little kindness.

It goes a long, long way lifting the spirit

like any early ray of sunshine.

It plants seeds of reciprocity, and those kind words

and pleasant actions can turn a heart of stone

into a rippling, effervescent fountain.

A person who is lonesome, depressed, and stumbling

in the darkness can emerge; lift himself up and be renewed

with vigor, and a new sense of purpose

by accepting a simple act of kindness.

A smile and a kind phrase can create little miracles,

and can be given out again and again.

The receiver is enriched, as is the receiver.

GIVE AWAY A SMILE

If you give away a smile it doesn't cost a penny.

The joy it brings is a gift for many.

If a person is in trouble and feeling sad,

you have the power to make them feel glad.

If you bestow on many a smiley face

you can bring happiness to the human race.

FOLLOW YOUR DREAMS

Sweep up your dreams

and put them in your pocket,

like a snip of hair

that fits in a locket.

You can put your dreams

on a pedestal to admire,

or infuse them with action

and achieve your desire.

Dreams that lie dormant

are often suppressed,

but dreams that are realized

are always the best.

REST

Go to sleep, do as you are bid.

Sleep will come upon you.

The soft sweet sleep, the peaceful rest.

Where as in a cocoon you

are softly protected from care,

and replenished with strength.

To awaken refreshed,

and ready for a new day.

MOOD SWINGS

Have you ever felt

so infinitesimal,

you wondered if

there was any worth

left in you,

wanting to curl up

into the tiniest ball

and disappear?

Yet there are other times

you feel so big that

your circumference

encompasses the entire world.

ONCE UPON A TIME

I walked the angelic gauntlet last night.

Truly in awe, amazement and wonder.

Walking with my eyes closed

angelic beings whispered sweet somethings

in my ears uplifting and endearing.

I was given love and amazing grace.

On the journey I surrendered myself

to the guardians,

and their endless devotion

who guided me on my journey.

Every fiber of my being

was made aware of the

angelic beings on my journey

and indeed I was blessed.

I cried out, thank you, thank you.

PART ELEVEN

SONGWRITING

In her twenties, Muriel wrote songs and music hoping to be recorded; they were a dream that never materialized. Here are six of her songs.

<u>THAT'S A WOMAN'S WAY</u>

A song written before marriage by Muriel Fischer in her early twen-
ties when she was interested in becoming a songwriter.

I've got my tongue in my cheek,

but I look shy and meek.

I'm sly as a fox,

but act dumb as an ox.

That's the way I gotta be

to keep my man loving me.

That's a woman's way.

He thinks I have no dough.

It don't hurt what he don't know.

I've got it stashed away.

In case he starts to stray.

That's the way it's got to be.

That's a woman's way.

To keep a man you gotta be smart

and you don't learn how at school.

You gotta be his little wife

and the angel in his life,

but at night be a loving fool.

let him think he's the boss,

without me he's really lost.

It cost me plenty of tears

and took me many years.

That's the way it's gotta be

to keep him loving me.

That's a woman's way.

<u>COME BACK TO PARADISE</u>

Come back to Paradise.

You have lingered too long.

Time stopped the day you went away.

Come back where you belong.

Come back to Paradise.

I'll forgive and forget.

Sweet memories of the love we knew are with me yet.

Let's rekindle the flame and

keep the love light burning.

It can still be the same without the yearning.

Come back to Paradise and

hear the angels sing.

My life is empty without you.

You are my everything.

Come back, come back to Paradise.

<u>MURDER OF LOVE</u>

Take two hearts filled with joy

a loving girl, a loving boy.

Enter a stranger, look out for danger.

Witness the murder of love.

Flirty eyes pass her by.

They're meant for Joey, you realize.

It's hard to know friend from foe.

Committing the murder of love.

To break a heart's a crime,

but who's to be the judge.

A broken heart's not worth a dime

in the courtroom of love.

Time will heal all the pain.

A new love's waiting

to play the game.

Have no regrets forgive and forget

all about the murder of love.

The murder of love.

I'M A TAR HEEL

I'm a Tar Heel, proud to be

living in the great state of NC.

When I look up at the Carolina sky

our future looks sunny, here's the reason why.

We're growing by leaps and bounds

new industries are moving to our cities and our towns.

We're showing a bright new face,

North Carolina's out to take first place.

I'm a Tar Heel, yes sir-ee

a genuine product of NC.

That's me -Tar Heel.

I WAS BORN TO BE LOVED

I was born to be loved,

but where is the guy who was born to love me.

I was born to be loved,

cooed, and turtle doved.

Can't you see my cup is running over.

To waste is a sin, I'm tired of being a rover,

Where is that certain him?

I was born to be loved.

I'm ready, willing and so very able.

I am ripe for the pick,

but where is the Tom, Jack and Dick.

Dear Lord up above, send me someone to love

someone to call my very own.

I was born to be loved, but how can I love all alone.

PLEASE GEORGE
Written for her true love and life partner.

Baby, oh baby, what should I do.

To make you realize that I love you.

I'm tired of carrying a torch,

why don't you satisfy my yearning.

Please George, rock and roll is the thing to do,

I'd like to rock and roll with you.

The sparks will fly, you will feel my torch.

Why don't you come a little closer?

Please George, you shouldn't be so so alone.

Affection is what you need.

If you will give me a chance,

I'll prove it to you, yes indeed.

ooh-ooh-ooh, I've got to go,

Boo hoo-boo hoo-I'll miss you so.

I'm so happy you took my advice

and it turned out very nice.

I'll meet you tomorrow on my front porch.

Now don't you disappoint me.

Please George!

PART TWELVE

FAMILY WRITINGS

A Book of Muriel's would be incomplete without family writings.

A MOTHER'S PRAYER

A mother's heartfelt prayer to protect her loved ones from harm.

Show him the way back.

Put him on the right path.

A Jewish girl, a Sabbath queen.

Only you can put him back

on the path he has fallen from.

Give him a sign.

Oh dear God, please

bring me back my son,

a man to be proud of.

For Yom Kippur,

I want him to be a

prince in the David tradition

worthy of his name.

IN CELEBRATION OF RIO

***Rio, the nickname for daughter Ellen who passed away
in her mid fifties from breast cancer.***

It wasn't meant to be this way.

I was supposed to go first,

but my shining star, my angel Rio

was taken from me.

She was my shining light,

my April 1st baby.

She is within my heart.

She walks with me, and is there

in my time of need.

I know heaven is beautified

when my angel Rio spreads her wings,

and rains down love to all of us here

and everywhere, making the world

a better place.

HAPPY BIRTHDAY CINDI AND STEVE

You both were born in Taurus—the sign of the bull.

You're not as stubborn as you used to be.

When the bull kicks up its heels,

I plead, "Please children stay away from me."

You both are kind, loving and giving.

You don't pinch pennies very tight,

I'm so happy that I am your Mom.

We're together celebrating tonight.

Let's see, should I order a drink.

A pina colada would be nice, oh well.

After ninety I deserve a drinkie

to make me feel slinky, loving and swell.

I'm so happy my adopted children,

Dan and Mariana are here too.

They're super and I love them so much.

Kids, let's keep celebrating

happy occasions together forever and ever.

Let's stay loving and in touch.

LOVE, LOVE, LOVE, MOM

SONG OF ESTHER LENA

Two short poems written upon the birth of her granddaughter.

A child is born.

A gift of God.

A miracle happens.

A dream is answered.

An awakening of the soul and spirit.

A vision of loveliness.

A child is born.

How fragrant thy breath.

How delightful thy touch.

How expressive thy hands.

I stand in awe and amazement.

My heart joins with that of my beloved.

How precious these moments.

Little darling, little princess.

LITTLE BIRD

For her mother Henrietta.

When the doctor said:

"Your mother is dying."

I cried out,

"Let us talk about living."

I prayed imaging you already healed.

I petitioned the Rabbis

to perform a miracle.

When the crises passed

the doctor marveled,

but Mamma you couldn't wait

for the healing.

I kindle the Sabbath lights,

say the blessing, see your face

in the flickering flames,

and remember how I used

to call you "Little Bird".

A GUTTE NESHAMA, 'A GOOD SOUL'
Muriel's mother-in-law Lena

You were always there for us

in the good time and the bad.

Sharing in our happiness

comforting us when we were sad.

You were peace and kindness

a gutte neshama.

You brought us out of darkness

with your light sense of humor.

Your memory will be a blessing

although now we may grieve.

Your good name and good deeds

is the heritage you leave.

MY WISH FOR YOU

My wishes are scattered like stars in

the heavens, wishes waiting to come true.

I wish for you success in your endeavors.

Lightness of spirit and gobs of golden

light to shine upon you.

I wish that in the bumps of life you land gently,

push yourself up and start again.

I wish you courage and steadfastness

to pursue your dreams, clearness of mind

to decipher your problems and solve them.

I wish you to know love, and for you to be

helpful in society to others less fortunate.

People need people and

you have a sweet loving nature.

I wish you patience, fortitude and

stick-with-it-ness to achieve your goals.

All this I wish you and many more.

With all my love,

Muriel